POCKET GUIDE TO
Sergers

T0269822

by Sue O'Very

POCKET GUIDE TO SERGERS

Landauer Publishing, www.landauerpub.com, is an imprint of Fox Chapel
Publishing Company, Inc.

Project Team
Managing Editor: Gretchen Bacon
Acquisitions Editor: Amelia Johanson
Editor: Christa Oestreich
Designer: Wendy Reynolds
Proofreader: Kurt Conley

ISBN 978-1-63981-097-0

Library of Congress Control Number: 2024942284

To learn more about the other great books from Fox Chapel Publishing,
or to find a retailer near you, call toll-free 800-457-9112,
send mail to
903 Square Street,
Mount Joy, PA 17552,
or visit us at www.FoxChapelPublishing.com.

We are always looking for talented authors. To submit an idea, please send a brief
inquiry to acquisitions@foxchapelpublishing.com.

Printed in China
First printing

Contents

Introduction 4

Who, What, Where, and Why 6

How To Choose the Right Serger for You? 9

Out of the Box 12

Parts and Pieces 15

Thread Stand 15

Threading 16

Threads 19

Tensions 25

Needles and Loopers 27

Width 29

Length 30

Feed Dogs and Differential Feed 31

Presser Foot, Presser Foot Lever, Knee Lift, and Pressure 33

Trim Bin 34

Types of Stitches: Overlock vs Coverstitch 36

Overlock Stitches 36

Coverstitch and Chainstitch 40

Combination Stitches 42

Feet and Accessories 43

Overlock Feet 44

Coverstitch Feet and Accessories 46

Get the Most Out of Your Serger 48

Start and Stop 48

Remove Stitches 51

Around Curves 52

Finish Ends 54

Notions that Make a Difference 55

Maintenance and Troubleshooting 58

Resources 62

About the Author 64

Introduction

The invention of the serger, or overlocker, more than 100 years ago transformed the fabric-finishing process by trimming and encapsulating edges with threads to prevent fraying, resulting in a polished, professional finish. In the 1960s, that sergers entered the home-sewing market, with every brand soon introducing their own version, revolutionizing home sewing.

Unlike traditional sewing machines, sergers operate without a bobbin. Instead, they utilize a combination of loopers moving side to side, reminiscent of crochet, and needles moving up and down to create overlock stitches. These stitches, aside from being practical and stretchy, can also offer decorative effects.

This book provides a foundational understanding of what a serger is, how it functions, the components involved, insights into threading, details about tensions, types of threads, common stitches, and how different presser feet can impact the machine's effectiveness.

A serger may resemble a sewing machine, but it offers so much more once you discover all its features.

Who, What, Where, and Why

A serger is an exquisite addition to any sewing room, catering to the needs of garment makers, bag creators, quilters, home-decor enthusiasts, and general sewers alike. For many, a sewing room feels incomplete without the presence of a serger.

Like the indispensable role of an oven in a kitchen, a sewing machine plays a crucial role in any sewing space by providing versatility in handling various stitches and sewing projects. On the other hand, a serger can be likened to a microwave; one acts as a valuable complement that speeds up cooking, the other in the swift and professional finishing of edges. While not a necessity for every sewing endeavor, a serger significantly enhances overall efficiency and convenience. Together, they create a harmonious duo, ensuring a well-equipped and streamlined sewing space.

The ideal candidate for a serger is someone prepared to elevate the quality and professionalism of their sewing creations. Owning a serger

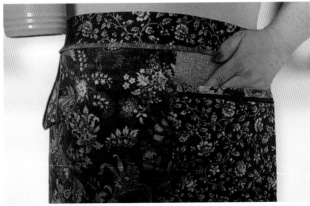

Sergers shine at creating polished seams, like the waistband on the Cookin' in Color Serger Apron, making them a must-have for any sewist.

offers the advantage of cutting and finishing edges on diverse materials, significantly improving durability and overall craftsmanship. The utility of a serger varies depending on the type of sewing one engages in.

Garment Makers

- Sergers excel in producing polished and professionally finished seams, making them indispensable for garment construction.
- They efficiently trim and finish fabric edges, preventing fraying.
- Sergers offer balanced stitches that can stretch, proving to be all-important for creating durable and flexible seams in garment construction.
- The use of flatlock, coverstitch, and chainstitch is ideal for working with knits, providing excellent results in hemming and seaming. Additionally, sergers offer numerous decorative applications.

A serger can easily create decorative stitches on bags, quilts, and other projects.

Bag Makers

- Crafters of bags can enhance seam and edge durability by utilizing a serger.
- For prequilted bags, finishing edges contribute to smooth, straight, and consistent seams.
- Sergers that offer piping feet that can help insert zippers, providing an ideal solution for bag makers.

Quilters

- Quilters often use sergers to finish fabric piece edges and create decorative seams.
- The machine's speed and efficiency are valuable for projects involving multiple quilt pieces.
- With a chainstitch, a serger can "quilt," sandwiching the front, back, and batting all together.
- Sergers are accurate and efficient for piecing, attaching the backing, quilting, and even binding.
- Use flatlock stitches to create crazy quilt blocks.
- Creating quilt-as-you-go quilts is fast and easy with either a 3-thread, 4-thread, or chainstitch.

Home-Decor Enthusiasts

- Those creating home-decor items, such as curtains, pillow covers, tablecloths, and napkins, can benefit from a serger for neat and durable seam finishes.
- Depending on the available presser feet, a serger allows the addition of zippers, piping, cording, beads, and other decorative trims.

General Sewers

- Individuals engaged in a broad spectrum of sewing projects can find a serger invaluable for adding a professional touch.
- Sergers are versatile tools capable of handling various fabrics and projects, from finishing edges before washing materials to quickly piecing materials together.
- It's good to know that a serger stitches almost twice as fast as your average sewing machine.

While not essential for every sewing task, a serger significantly enhances overall efficiency and professionalism in completed projects.

HOW TO CHOOSE THE RIGHT SERGER FOR YOU?

Once you've made the decision to invest in a serger, the next step is to conduct thorough research to identify the machine that best suits your specific needs. Several factors come into play when making this decision:

Budget: Determine your budget range. Sergers are available at various price points, from a couple hundred to several thousand dollars, so having a clear budget will help streamline your options. At the same time, don't miss out on an opportunity to get a serger with more options if it is slightly over your budget.

Type of Projects: Consider the type of sewing projects you plan to undertake. Different sergers come with features tailored to specific fabrics and projects. Inquire about the motor's capability and its performance when stitching through heavier materials.

Stitch Options: Sergers come in 4-thread, 5-thread variations (some brands offer more thread options), stand-alone chain/coverstitch, or combo (overlock and coverstitch in one machine). While all, minus the stand-alone chain/coverstitch, can handle basic overlock stitches, some may offer additional stitches for decorative or specialized purposes. Don't overlook features like differential feed, knee lift, presser foot height (some sergers offer extra height), speed control (some sergers have computerized speed control), extension tables, pressure control, trim bin, and wider cutting widths (which can open the door to even more decorative and functional use).

Knowing what accessories are offered for each serger, such as these for the coverstitch, is an important factor to consider when choosing the right machine for you.

Take advantage of serger classes offered by your dealer. I've taught hundreds of events nationwide.

Ease of Threading and Tensions: Threading a serger and adjusting tensions can be challenging. Look for models with color-coded threading guides, built-in help guides, threading charts, or air-threading systems for easier setup. Additionally, consider sergers with automatic tension adjustments or computerized tensions, and ideally, a combination of both for personalized control.

Extra Feet and Accessories: Confirm the availability of the most popular presser feet and accessories for the machines you are considering. For example, some sergers offer various sizes of piping feet. Even within a single brand, not all machines have access to the same feet and accessories. It's crucial to conduct thorough research before making a purchase. Ask the questions now so you know what to expect.

Brands and Reviews: Research different brands and read user reviews. Joining online sewing communities, such as Facebook groups, can also provide valuable insights. Established and reputable brands often produce high-quality machines and offer extended educational resources through blogs, social media, and online videos. Remember, when you invest a significant sum for a serger, ensure it aligns with your preferences and requirements for the long haul.

Dealer Support and Warranty: Buy from a reputable dealer offering good customer support, classes, servicing, and knowledge of the machine you intend to buy. Check the manufacturer's warranty; most come with a one year on parts and labor. However, it's a good idea to ask about the dealer warranty, as you'll probably need to bring the machine in for servicing after the one-year manufacturer warranty runs out.

Test before Buying: Ask the salesperson for a demonstration, as it can likely address many of your questions. Furthermore, inquire if your local store offers rental options or classes where you can use the machine for a day. Alternatively, consider participating in a designer event where you can work on a project and thoroughly test the machine. If you have specific materials you intend to use frequently, bring along scraps to test how well the serger handles them.

By considering these factors, you can narrow down your options and find a serger that perfectly aligns with your sewing needs and preferences.

Choosing the right serger will save you time and money while ensuring a smooth and enjoyable stitching experience.

Out of the Box

Often in conversations about sergers with fellow sewing enthusiasts, I frequently hear statements like, "I own a serger, but it's still in the box," or even worse, "It's out of the box but tucked away in the closet." Let's admit it, the prospect of dealing with multiple threads, tensions, needles, and loopers can make a serger seem quite daunting. Consequently, many of these machines are purchased, brought home, perhaps unpacked, only to find their way into the closet, leaving the owner with the all-too-familiar sense of buyer's remorse. By the end of this book, my hope is that you'll not only retrieve your serger from its box but also place it on your table and confidently start stitching with it.

Speaking of tables, when considering where to position your serger, think about using a sturdy table that can absorb vibrations. Sergers operate at speeds ranging from 600 to 1400 stitches per minute, depending on the make and model. If you're fortunate enough to have a dedicated sewing space, height-adjustable tables or a customized cabinet with cutouts designed to accommodate your serger at the perfect height could be ideal. Adjustable tables provide the flexibility to sew or serge while standing

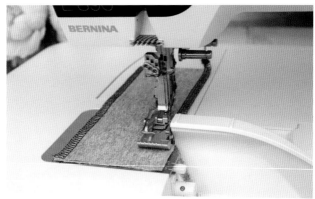

Once you get the hang of using a serger to finish seams, you'll never want to go back to the old way.

Some sergers have a smaller base to insert round items, like cuffs, making it easy to finish "in the round."

or sitting, promoting comfort for your back and upper shoulders. On the other hand, if you're bringing your serger out of the closet to place it on the kitchen table, ensure that it rests on a flat, even surface. There are foam mats you can purchase that are designed to help absorb high-speed vibrations of the serger, and these also help keep an uneven table surface flat.

It never ceases to amaze me how many people invest in sergers but never fully utilize them. Often, this underutilization is due to a lack of education, and when it comes to sergers, education is paramount for mastering these machines. Your serger will come with some form of a user manual. Nowadays, many high-end sergers have built-in computerized manuals, while others may rely exclusively on online resources—be sure to inquire about this before making your purchase.

When buying a serger, I typically recommend buying from a local dealer who offers basic education with the option for ongoing classes that involve serger projects. This package usually includes a few lessons, possible participation in a monthly club, and most importantly, servicing for your machine.

For those purchasing a serger online, whether new or used, it's crucial to consider where and how you'll receive your education and service. Will a local dealer provide education for a machine bought online from another source? If so, be prepared to potentially pay a premium for your education, as it is often included with the cost of a machine at a local shop. Additionally, inquire about the warranty, as most machines come with a one-year manufacturer's warranty on parts; however, labor typically is not included.

Most manufacturers offer user-friendly websites with extensive educational resources, projects, and downloadable workbooks. Many also have YouTube channels, and some maintain blogs featuring designers who showcase their machines with free projects to demonstrate serger techniques. One example is WeAllSew, the BERNINA and bernette blog (see Resources).

Furthermore, several serger pattern designers, myself included, post videos online, offer video courses, and have serger-based projects that delve into machine settings, presser feet, unique threads, and techniques—all valuable for continuing your learning journey. Refer to the Resources page for more information.

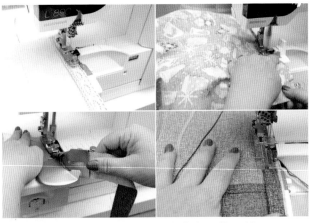

Sergers can evenly attach lace, clean finish an edge, attaching binding, and insert piping.

Parts and Pieces

Sergers showcase innovation with intricate design that include various moving components, blades, and multiple needles. When precisely aligned, they can produce highly professional results. Understanding the basics of their diverse parts and features will be helpful as you get to know your serger. While variations exist between brands and models, certain fundamental components are common to all sergers. Moreover, higher-end sergers may feature additional bonus capabilities. The goal of this section is to offer a comprehensive analysis of each component, including a discussion on threads and needles.

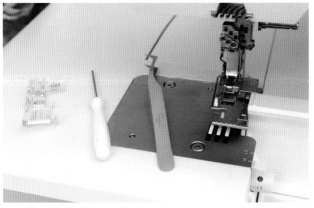

Left to right: clear overlock foot, screwdriver with a hex head, angled precision tweezers, and standard foot.

THREAD STAND

A serger thread stand is a device designed to hold and dispense multiple spools of thread for a serger. Sergers typically have multiple threads running concurrently, and a thread stand helps organize and manage these threads during the stitching process. The stand usually has several vertical rods or pegs, each capable of holding a separate spool of thread with a telescopic guide rising above and behind the thread cones, so the thread can easily feed off the cone and into the tension disc. This arrangement allows the threads to feed smoothly into the serger without tangling or getting in the way.

Thread stands contribute to the overall efficiency and functionality of a serger by providing a convenient and organized way to handle the various threads required for different stitching techniques. The thread stand not only organizes the thread to ensure smooth flow, but it is also crucial to adhere to the thread chart. This is because, frequently, the spools are positioned on specific pegs to ensure precise tension delivery.

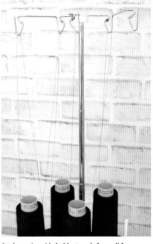

A telescopic guide holds strands from all four thread cones below, keeping them separate and organized.

THREADING

Threading a serger may initially seem daunting, but with familiarity and practice, it becomes a matter of muscle memory. Unlike a conventional sewing machine with a single thread on top and a small bobbin below, a serger involves managing multiple spools at the top of the machine. Each spool must be threaded in the correct order with precision. Fortunately, most machines provide color-coded guides, detailed diagrams, and even tweezers to assist in intricate threading locations. Many brands also offer instructional videos on their websites or YouTube channels to guide users through the threading process, not to mention various designers' online videos.

It's worth mentioning that some machines on the market feature air threading, where a single thread is placed inside a designated metal thread port, and a burst of air guides the thread tail to the exact location needed.

Manual Threading

When a serger is labeled as manual threading or manually threaded, it indicates that users are required to personally guide and thread each thread through the designated paths and components of the serger, following a specific order. This stands in contrast to the automated or air-threading features that will be covered in the next section. The process entails a thorough review of the user manual or threading chart. Tools like tweezers may be used to navigate intricate threading paths. Although it might require some practice and time investment, this manual threading approach offers users a high level of control over their threads, including the use of various decorative thread options.

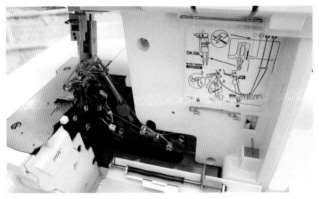

Many sergers will come with an on-machine threading manual.

Air Threading

An air-threading serger, also known as automatic or self-threading, represents a type of serger equipped with an innovative threading mechanism designed to streamline and quicken the threading process. The first time I encountered an air-threading serger, it felt like witnessing a magic show. In contrast to traditional sergers that demand manual threading through various guides and paths, air-threading sergers utilize an air-driven system to assist in seamlessly threading the threads through the machine. The air-threading process typically involves the following steps:

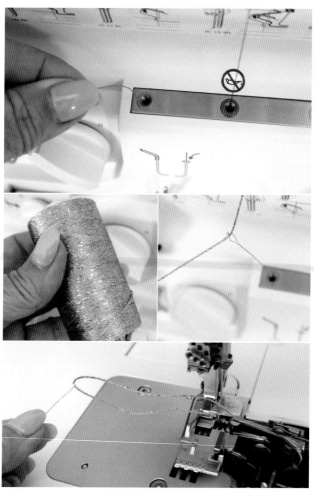

Top: Thread goes into a thread port. Middle and bottom: Wire threaders are used for heavier threads.

1. **Thread Port:** The user places the thread into a designated thread port on the machine and "engages the thread ports" by sliding over a lever.
2. **Air Assistance:** With the touch of a button or in some cases, pressing the foot controller, a burst of air is generated by the machine. This helps guide the thread through the intricate threading path (thread port) to the exact location needed.
3. **Automatic Threading:** The serger's air-threading system automates the process of threading the upper and lower loopers, and the chain looper for combination machines.

It's important to note that the air-threading feature is exclusively applied to the loopers, while the needles are threaded manually. Some machines may provide a manual threading tool, and certain sergers offer a built-in needle threader as an additional convenience.

Air-threading sergers may weigh more, have a larger footprint, and be more expensive compared to their manually threaded counterparts. Depending on the make and model, the user might find threading thicker decorative threads through the thread ports more difficult. The manufacturers are aware of this and most include a thread wire, a thin metal wire with a loop at one end. You will engage the thread port, feed the thin wire into it, and feed the thicker thread into the loop end, pulling it through the thread port. The process is quite easy and efficient.

THREADS

In terms of thread selection, sergers accommodate various types, ranging from standard to decorative threads. Exploring the possibilities with different threads can reveal the full potential of your machine. This exploration allows for the discovery of new capabilities, adding a touch of magic to your sewing projects.

Standard Threads

Serger thread is finer than most threads and commonly made from polyester or a polyester blend. The fine nature of serger thread helps reduce bulk in the seams created by the overlock stitch. You might be wondering if you can use standard sewing thread on a serger—the short answer is yes, but there are a few things to keep in mind. My go-to standard serger thread is Mettler SERACOR, which is 50wt, because of its smooth finish and consistent stitch quality.

A fine polyester thread is ideal for a serger.

Thread Weight: Thread comes in various weights (thicknesses), denoted by numbers. The thicker the thread, the smaller the number (8wt is heavy). The thinner the thread, the larger the number (60wt is very fine). The thicker thread will create bulkier seams when used on a serger and might even appear to be stiffer, which might not yield professional results.

Fiber Content: While sewing thread can be made from various materials like cotton, polyester, or nylon, serger thread is often made from polyester or a polyester blend. Using a sewing thread with a similar fiber content to serger thread is advisable for consistent results. If you plan to do quilt piecing with your serger, you might consider using a thinner cotton thread. Ask your local dealer for recommendations.

Tension Adjustment: When switching from serger thread to sewing thread, or vice versa, you may need to adjust the tension settings on your serger. Different threads may require slight tension adjustments to achieve the desired stitch quality.

Consider the Project: For projects where the bulk of the seam is a concern, such as lightweight fabrics or tight-fitting garments, using a finer sewing thread on the serger may be more appropriate.

While using sewing thread on a serger is possible, keep in mind that serger thread is specifically designed for overlock machines, providing optimal results in terms of stitch quality, stretch, and durability. Experimenting with different threads and making tension adjustments will help you achieve the desired outcome for your specific project.

Decorative Threads

Integrating decorative threads into your serger projects brings about distinctive and creative elements. A variety of decorative thread types, including rayon, polyester, cotton, metallic, and specialty blends, provides a wide array of options. Many of these threads can be used in both the loopers and needles of a serger, although certain accessories like a larger needle, thread stand, nets, or spool pins may be required. Most of these types of threads have a variegated collection; check with your local dealer or look on various thread companies' websites.

Adjusting tensions might be necessary when working with different stitch types and threads. When working with decorative threads in a serger, it's recommended to experiment and enjoy the process, making notes along the way. Some sergers even allow you to memorize stitches, offering the opportunity to name unique stitch and thread combinations. Additionally, you can have fun experimenting with thread blending by feeding two or more threads through a looper or the eye of the needle. Note there are aftermarket thread stands designed to help the tensions remain consistent.

Because a serger can incorporate multiple thread colors in one stitch, you may want to experiment with decorative threads.

Machine Embroidery Thread:
Typically, this thread is rayon or polyester and usually 40wt. It is suggested to use an aftermarket thread stand, such as Thread Fusion by Gail Patrice Design, to ensure the tension is properly delivered for consistent stitches. It might be useful to use a thread net. Thread blending is very nice with embroidery thread since it is thin, smooth, and can be used in both the loopers and needles.

Machine embroidery thread is a lighter option.

Metallic Thread: Metallic thread is usually blended with another fiber, typically polyester or nylon, which is then wrapped or coated with a thin layer of metallic foil or film. Ranging from 8wt to 40wt thread, it allows for the appearance of a metallic shine while maintaining flexibility and ease of use in sewing machines and sergers. The heavier-weight metallic threads specially designed with sergers in mind, such as GlaMore™ 12wt and Dazzle™ 8wt (both from WonderFil), provide stunning results when used in the upper loopers.

Metallic thread is slightly more substantial, offers a fun challenge, and adds a beautiful sparkle.

It is suggested to use a thread net for even delivery, as metallic thread tends to twist while coming off the cone or spool. Check with your local dealer for optional thread stands or guides when using this type of thread. If you plan to use the thread in the eye of the needle, it is suggested to increase the needle size for 90/14, allowing for the thread to glide through more evenly.

Untextured Thread: Untextured serger thread is characterized by its smooth, soft, and fluffy texture, often referred to as "wooly," stemming from the original offering, wooly nylon. This type of thread maintains a nice, smooth, and consistent coverage, instantly imparting a professional

Untextured thread is smooth, perfect for garment construction.

finish to the work. While the original wooly nylon was made of nylon, which isn't ideal for pressing, numerous brands now offer untextured threads in polyester. This type of serger thread is particularly favored for achieving clean and smooth seams, making it a common choice in garment construction, finishing rolled hems, and wide overlock on fleece.

This thread typically doesn't require a thread net, as it flows off the cone evenly without twisting. If you plan to use it through the eye of the needle, experiment with a larger-eye needle if you have any skipped stitches. Threads shown above are from the Sookie Sews "Fluffy Bee" collection of SoftLoc™ thread from WonderFil.

Corded Thread: This 8wt thread is often referred to as "twisted," such as Pearl Crown Rayon by Y.L.I. This thread is a lustrous, densely twisted rayon thread with substantial thickness, ideal for creating exquisite serged edges, flatlock stitches in the needle or loopers, and chain/coverstitches on the chain looper. It is suggested to use a thread net for even delivery as this type of thread tends to twist while coming off the cone or spool.

Corded thread is heavier but great for serged edges.

Check with your local dealer for optional thread stands or guides when using this type of thread. If you plan to use it in the eye of the needle, it is suggested to increase the needle size for 90/14, allowing for the thread to glide through more evenly. It should also be noted that this thread is typically rayon and is not colorfast, so be mindful of future washing and potential bleeding.

Cotton Thread: This 12wt thread is smooth and glides through your serger in the loopers and needle. When threading through the eye of the needle, opt for an 80/12 serger needle. However, if you encounter threading difficulties, switch to a larger size, such as a 90/14 serger needle. No net is required, as it evenly feeds off the spool. This thread is ideal for thread blending when you combine two or more threads through one looper; however, consider using an aftermarket thread stand like Thread Fusion by Gail Patrice Design to ensure the tension is properly delivered for consistent stitches.

My favorite 12wt cotton is an Egyptian cotton called Spagetti™ from WonderFil. I personally refer to this thread as a "magic thread." It seems no matter which stitch I use in the needle, loopers, rolled hem, chain/coverstitch, and even the basic 4-thread overlock, it works consistently every single time, like magic! Threads shown below are from the Sookie Sews "The Beehive" collection of Spagetti thread from WonderFil.

Cotton thread is perfect for combining colors.

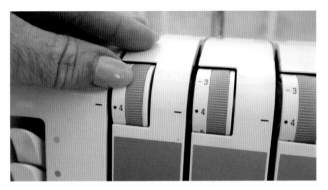

Machine with manual tension dials allow for tension to be adjusted on each thread.

TENSIONS

Properly adjusted tension ensures that the serger stitches are strong, durable, and aesthetically pleasing. This can be achieved on a serger through manual means, by adjusting dials, or automatically by the machine deciding for you. No matter which you choose, the most important factor is to get balanced stitches.

Manual: Manual tensions on a serger are the adjustable dials that determine the tightness or looseness of the threads during the stitching process. A higher tension number indicates tighter tension, while a lower number signifies looser tension. With manual tension controls, users can set the tension for each thread individually. The adjustment of these tensions is crucial in achieving well-balanced and properly formed stitches. Optimal tension ensures that the threads interlock effectively, resulting in strong and even seams. When working with different thread types or weights, manual tension adjustments may be necessary to attain the desired stitch quality.

Referring to your serger's manual is essential for precise instructions on adjusting tensions, given that different serger models may feature slightly varied mechanisms for tension control. Additionally, experimenting with scrap fabric allows for practice in finding the right tension settings for different projects and thread combinations.

Screen showing automatic tensions set by choosing the stitch, but the user can adjust them as well.

Automatic: Automatic tension on a serger is a feature found in certain makes and models that eliminates the necessity for manual tension adjustments. Instead of manually configuring tension dials for each thread, the serger incorporates an automatic tension system. This system adapts tensions based on factors like thread type, thickness, and the chosen stitch. On sergers with automatic tension, it's crucial to precisely position the thread cones on the stand, taking note of the specific thread guide and tension disc for each.

While automatic tension systems offer a time-saving convenience, experienced sewers may still prefer manual control for fine-tuning tensions in specific situations. The availability and complexity of automatic-tension features can vary among serger models, particularly in computerized models where tensions adjust automatically, yet users retain the ability to fine-tune. Some view this as an ideal combination, a win-win. Always consult your serger's manual for precise instructions on the operation of the automatic tension system in your machine.

How To Get Balanced Stitches: Ensuring balanced stitches on a serger is essential to achieving tidy and professional seams. Balanced stitches are attained when the tension for each looper thread—both upper and lower—is correctly adjusted, resulting in a uniform, interlocked stitch. The needles too must be set to the preferred tension, so the thread lies nice and flat. After testing the stitch with the specific thread-and-fabric combination,

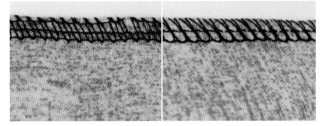

You can tell when stitches come out uneven by the top looping down into the fabric (left). The curved stitch should run along the top edge (right).

if imbalance persists, carefully review the threading path and tensions, ensure new needles are installed at the highest position, and consult the user manual for guidance, which is often accompanied by diagrams.

As a general rule, if the upper looper stitches are pulling toward the back, consider loosening the lower looper tension and/or tightening the upper looper tension. Test the stitch again. A useful approach is to adjust while actively stitching, allowing you to observe real-time changes in the stitch appearance.

NEEDLES AND LOOPERS

As previously mentioned in this guide, sergers function without a bobbin. They employ a combination of loopers (upper, lower, and chain) that move side to side, while needles go up and down to create stitches. Consult the user manual for the appropriate needle type on your machine, but most sergers use the ELx705 needle. This needle features a second groove that reduces friction, making it suitable for thicker materials, higher speeds, and bulkier threads. Additionally, check with your local dealer

Loopers are found to the right of the needles, presser foot, and blade.

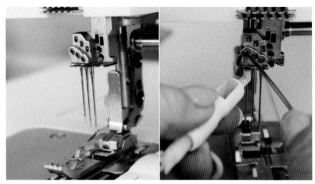

Depending on the stitch, sergers can use several needles at the same time.

for alternative needle options, as many sergers can also accommodate universal, stretch, jeans, and metallic needles just to name a few.

Two important considerations regarding serger needles: ensure they are at the highest position, which can be challenging due to the proximity of multiple needles; and confirm that the needle screws are fully tightened. Despite their small size, these screws are critical, and any looseness can lead to potential damage or loss during rapid serging. Plus, remember that sergers stitch very fast, and these high speeds can cause a loose needle to fall out. If you happen to lose a needle or screw during stitching, it's important to calmly locate it before continuing. Loose parts within the serger's internal components can potentially cause damage to the machine, so it's best to secure them promptly.

As needles move up and down, loopers move side to side, and whether you have an overlock, chain/coverstitch, or combo machine, each plays a role in stitch formation. The upper looper creates stitches on the top of the fabric, while the lower looper forms stitches on the bottom. The chain looper is responsible for the lower edge stitching in chain or coverstitches. Some machines offer a bypass option for air-threading sergers, allowing the use of threads too thick for the thread ports. Utilizing this feature varies between machines, so refer to the user manual or threading chart for specific instructions.

WIDTH

When discussing overlock on a serger, width pertains to the space between the left needle and the cutting blade or knife that trims the fabric. By adjusting the width setting, you can reposition the blade: lower numbers shift it to the left, nearer to the needle(s), resulting in a narrower width; higher numbers move the blade to the right, yielding a wider width. Most sergers allow width adjustments ranging from 3mm to 5mm, with newer models offering even broader options, extending up to 9mm. This array of settings provides a wide range of stitching possibilities across different widths.

Another factor affecting width is the stitch finger adjustment. Typically, sergers feature three stitch fingers positioned beneath the presser foot to the right of the feed dogs, precisely aligned under the needles. Stitch fingers play a crucial role in creating flat, balanced stitches. While the far-left and center stitch fingers remain stationary, the far-right finger moves side to side, usually in tandem with the blade's movement, which is what creates the stitch width. When the third stitch finger is removed, this creates the narrowest hem, most often used to create a rolled hem commonly seen on napkin edges.

The blade on an overlock machine can cut fabric to the desired size.

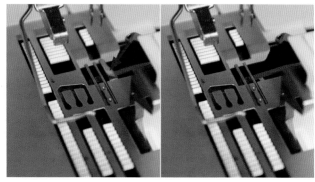

Two of the stitch fingers remain in place while the third is adjustable. Notice the far-right finger is in place (left) and is removed (right).

Certain specialty stitches found on newer machines, like narrow overlock and picot stitches, also require the removal of this stitch finger. Given that the far-left and middle stitch fingers remain fixed, they often go unnoticed, with references in manuals or instructions simply denoting them as "stitch fingers." Necessary stitch finger adjustments are typically indicated by a rolled-hem option or selector on the machine, labeled as rolled (R) or overlock (O). The user manual or threading/stitch chart specifies whether to engage the (R) or (O) selector for different stitching needs.

LENGTH

Similar to a sewing machine, stitch length on a serger denotes the distance between consecutive points where the needles and loopers penetrate the fabric to create a stitch. Various components, including the differential feed, contribute to the overall variability of a serger's moving parts.

Typically measured in millimeters, adjusting the stitch length on a serger provides control over the appearance and characteristics of the stitches. Common settings may range from very short, 0.5mm for tight and secure seams, to longer, 2.5–4.5mm for a looser and more flexible seam. Stitch length is just one factor influencing the final stitch appearance on a serger. Thread tension, differential feed, thread type, fabric type, and

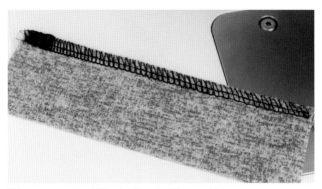

It's important to recognize stitch length, as it's one factor in a successful seam.

the chosen stitch type also contribute to the overall outcome of the serged seam. For precise guidance on adjusting and comprehending stitch-length settings, refer to your serger's manual, which provides specific instructions tailored to your machine.

FEED DOGS AND DIFFERENTIAL FEED

Feed dogs, the toothed mechanisms situated beneath the presser foot, play a vital role in propelling the fabric forward during stitching. In older or budget sergers, only one set of feed dogs is present, similar to those seen on a sewing machine. However, sergers equipped with a differential feed feature have two sets of feed dogs—one positioned in front of the other. These sets move at varying speeds, gathering or stretching the fabric.

The ratio between the front and back feed dogs can be adjusted using the serger's controls for differential feed, affecting only the front set of feed dogs. This attribute proves particularly advantageous in preventing fabric from stretching or puckering, especially when dealing with knits or stretchy materials.

Typically, the differential feed can be set between 0.7 and 2.0, with the neutral setting at 1.0. A lower number indicates that the front feed dogs take shorter steps, moving slower, essentially stretching the material. Conversely, a higher number suggests that the front feed dogs take longer steps, moving faster than the back feed dogs, resulting in either gathering

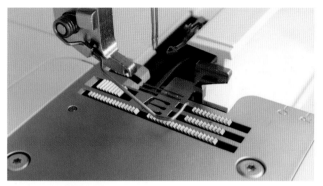

Feed dogs move your fabric along.

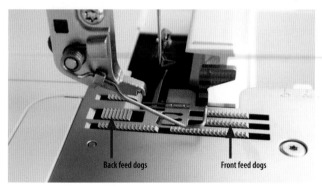

Back feed dogs   Front feed dogs

The difference between front and back feed dogs is differential.

the fabric or preventing knits from stretching too much. For precise instructions on adjusting the differential feed for various sewing scenarios, always refer to your serger's manual.

PRESSER FOOT, PRESSER FOOT LEVER, KNEE LIFT, AND PRESSURE

Left: The standard presser foot works with the feed dogs to guide the fabric forward. Right: There is a lever to raise and lower the presser foot.

Like a sewing machine, a serger is equipped with a presser foot. This is a crucial component that secures the fabric in place during the stitching process. Positioned at the front of the serger, the presser foot collaborates with the feed dogs to guide the fabric through the machine. Most sergers include the standard presser foot, offering a variety of specialty feet that will snap on/off to the shank. The presser foot lever, typically located behind the presser foot, raises and lowers the foot, allowing for the insertion of fabric. In certain makes and models, this lever may be positioned on the side of the machine; refer to the user manual.

Some sergers feature built-in knee lifts, also known as hands-free systems. A knee lift is a mechanical feature that enables users to raise and lower the presser foot using their knee, eliminating the need to use their hands to

The presser foot lever comes on every serger to raise and lower the foot.

The pressure dial determines how much force is put on your fabric.

lift the presser-foot lever. This proves beneficial when pivoting or adjusting the fabric with both hands during stitching, the knee lift is referred to as a third hand. It's a wonderful addition to a serger. Just make sure you have space under the table it is positioned on to take full advantage of it.

Pressure pertains to the force applied by the presser foot onto the fabric being stitched. This force is crucial for achieving optimal stitch quality and ensuring the fabric moves smoothly through the serger.

A knee lift is useful for raising the presser foot when your hands are already occupied.

Most modern sergers can adjust the dial up and down to either add more pressure or decrease the amount of pressure. The general rule is the lower the number, the less pressure; the higher the number, the more pressure.

TRIM BIN

The trim bin on a serger is designed to effectively handle and gather surplus fabric, thread, and trimmings produced during the serging process. Positioned on or near the serger, this small container or compartment captures the cut edges and waste materials resulting from the machine's trimming and fabric-finishing actions. The design and placement of trim bins vary based on the specific serger model. Some sergers come equipped with built-in bins or trays, while others offer attachments or accessories with a similar purpose. Regardless of the configuration, the trim bin contributes to the overall efficiency and user convenience of a serger by minimizing the mess generated during the cutting and finishing stages of the sewing process.

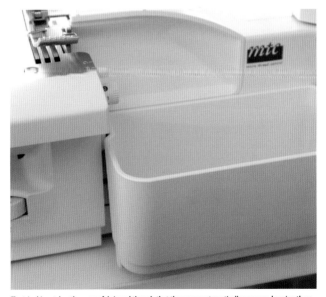

The trim bin catches the excess fabric and threads that the serger automatically removes, keeping them out of your work.

Types of Stitches:
Overlock vs Coverstitch

Serger stitches can be divided into two primary categories: overlock and coverstitch. The specific stitches offered may vary based on the machine's features and capabilities. Nevertheless, our focus in this section will be on basic serger stitches. For a comprehensive list of available serger stitches and instructions on how to execute them, please refer to your user manual. Although overlock and coverstitch machines have traditionally been sold separately, a rising trend involves combination machines that empower users to produce both types of stitches. These machines introduce a third category known as combination stitches, which incorporate both chainstitch and overlock capabilities.

OVERLOCK STITCHES

The humble overlock stitch is created using at least one needle moving vertically, complemented by two loopers operating horizontally to form the distinctive overlock stitch. As the needles ascend and descend, a blade

A serger can create a variety of stitches that are for both function and decoration.

trims the fabric edge, while the looper threads gracefully envelop the edge, yielding a polished, professional finish. Remarkably, the overlock stitch offers a spectrum of possibilities, with certain machines on the market capable of generating numerous stitch combinations. This versatility is achieved by adjusting variables like the number of needles, threads, tensions, and loopers. The prospect of creating a myriad of stitches on a machine initially designed solely for finishing fabric edges is truly extraordinary. In the following sections, we will explore the four most-prevalent types of overlock stitches.

Overlock Wide

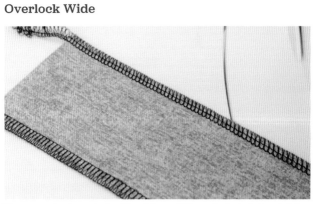

To create a classic overlock wide stitch, you'll insert both the left and right needles along with both upper and lower loopers, utilizing a total of four threads. This stitch variant is often referred to as a 4-thread overlock wide, or simply a 4-thread overlock. Generally favored, it's suitable for medium- to heavy-weight fabrics.

Alternatively, you can omit the right needle while retaining both upper and lower loopers. This variation, known as a 3-thread overlock wide or 3-thread overlock, is perfect for lighter- to medium-weight materials. The decision between a 3-thread and 4-thread overlock hinges on fabric characteristics, project specifications, and desired outcomes. If unsure which stitch to use in a project, test them both out to see which performs better.

Overlock Narrow

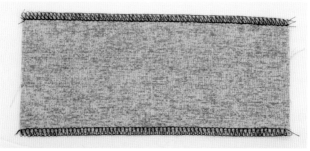

Similar to the overlock wide, the overlock narrow will involve both the upper and lower loopers; however, in this case, only the right needle is used. A 3-thread overlock narrow is particularly useful for light- to medium-weight fabrics where reducing bulk is important, such as in garment construction, finishing raw edges, or creating decorative edges on lightweight fabrics. Additionally, it can be utilized for hemming or seaming delicate fabrics where a wider stitch may be too conspicuous or excessive.

Rolled Hem

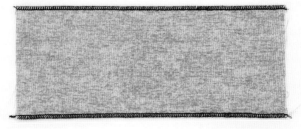

When picturing a rolled hem, one often imagines the beautifully finished hem on elegant cloth napkins. This stitching technique is particularly well-suited for delicate fabrics like chiffon and silk but are widely used on the edge of lightweight knits.

Similar to the 3-thread overlock, the rolled-hem technique exclusively utilizes the right needle along with both upper and lower loopers. The primary distinction lies in adjusting the stitch fingers. As discussed earlier, there are three stitch fingers. While the far-left and center fingers stay fixed, facilitating the formation of balanced stitches, removing the far right stitch finger causes the upper looper to wrap around to the back side of the stitch, resulting in the characteristic "rolled" effect. Tension adjustments are crucial, so unless your machine automatically manages tensions, it's advisable to consult your user manual. Many machines can achieve a 2-thread rolled hem, a lovely delicate stitch, so it's worth checking your serger settings and user manual for this option.

Flatlock

Unlike the overlock stitch, the flatlock stitch doesn't require turning the seam toward either side upon completion. Instead, the seam is opened, causing each side of the seam allowance to lie flat on top of the other. One side exhibits a flat, ladder-like appearance (resulting from the needle thread), while the other side showcases a distinctive squiggly seam (created by the looper thread). This technique produces a flat seam, minimizing bulk and giving rise to the term "flatlock."

A flatlock stitch can be executed with two or three threads, depending on the desired width, style, and tensions. This method is commonly used in the construction of sportswear, where a smooth, flat seam is preferred, such as activewear, swimwear, and undergarments.

COVERSTITCH AND CHAINSTITCH

Both coverstitches and chainstitches are produced using a specialized machine known as a coverstitch machine. The primary distinction between a coverstitch and an overlock machine lies in the absence of a blade that cuts the material, though many sergers offer both options in one machine. Similar to a sewing machine, there is a flat table beneath the needle and presser foot, providing a surface for the fabric and stitches to rest flat.

A typical coverstitch machine offers three needle options, usually referred to as chain needles. Instead of two loopers moving from side to side to encase the threads around the fabric's edge, the coverstitch machine features a single looper, referred to as the chain looper, that functions more like a bobbin. The chain looper catches the needle threads and lays the thread combination flat.

Coverstitch

The coverstitch involves utilizing two or more chain needles and the chain looper. When applied, the needle stitches are visible on the top side of the fabric, while the bottom side displays the effect of the looper thread. This method is commonly employed to secure hems in knit garments. For an example, examine the hem of a T-shirt, where two evenly spaced needle stitches are apparent on the top side. Flipping the hem to the bottom side reveals a distinctive squiggly line—a result of the looper thread skillfully "covering" the raw edge. This defining characteristic is what gives the technique its name, coverstitch.

Chainstitch

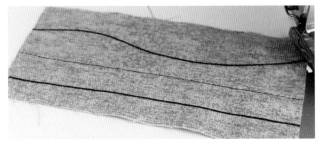

A subset of the coverstitch category is the chainstitch, characterized by a single needle on the fabric's top and a thin loopy stitch on the back. When thinking of a chainstitch, one might be reminded of the annoying thread on a bag of oranges. Properly clipping the thread allows for easy bag opening, but if not done precisely, you may need to cut the top of the bag off in frustration. In the chapter "Remove Stitches" (page 51), you'll discover how simple it is to remove chainstitches when you know which threads to clip and exactly where. In modern serging, the chainstitch gets a lot of use with construction, decorative stitching, or even as a quilting stitch to sandwich layers of materials together.

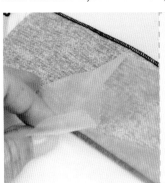

PRO TIP

When stitching a rolled hem on the bias or around a curve, you might see fibers poking out. Try placing a piece of wash-away stabilizer, such as Sulky Solvy, over the fabric edge. Cut both the fabric and stabilizer at the same time. Once finished stitching and cutting, remove the remaining stabilizer. This will help smooth out the poking fibers.

Use wash-away stabilizer to keep fibers form escaping the rolled hem.

COMBINATION STITCHES

Some sergers have the ability to create both overlock and coverstitch on the same machine by carefully switching settings, feet, needle position, and more. It is like having two machines in one. Many consumers opt for this version of a serger, since now there is only one machine in their sewing room, plus the addition of more stitch options. In addition to being able to stitch overlock and coverstitch on one machine, you now have the advantage of combination stitches like chainstitch + overlock among many others.

Chainstitch + Overlock

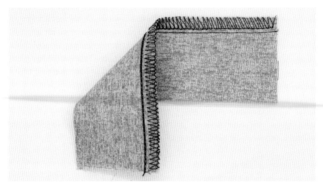

The combination of chainstitch and overlock stitches is a process that engages a varied combination of the upper and lower loopers, the chain looper, and needles on both the coverstitch and overlock sides of the machine. Premium sergers often provide numerous variations of this stitch, not only for functionality, but also for decorative purposes. This particular combination stitch finds frequent use in garment construction, where the chainstitch serves as the construction stitch, while the overlock stitch functions as the finishing touch.

Feet and Accessories

Just as presser feet and accessories enhance the functionality of a sewing machine, they also broaden the capabilities of a serger, extending its basic functions. However, the availability of these accessories may vary depending on the brand and model of the serger. Even within the same brand, not all feet are interchangeable due to differences in needle positions. Therefore, it's essential to familiarize yourself with the specific offerings of your serger when considering additional accessories.

When exploring the range of feet and accessories available, take note of those that pique your interest, particularly when contemplating your first or next serger purchase. Personally, I find brands that offer a variety of features and accessories appealing, as they indicate potential for growth and versatility in the future. Throughout my journey with sergers, I've discovered that certain models offer extra feet and accessories, which sparked my curiosity to explore their capabilities further. It is also worth mentioning that, just like many sewing machine presser feet, there is an added cost to serger feet and accessories.

In this chapter, I aim to cover as many feet and accessories as possible based on the machine I own at the time of writing this book, the BERNINA L 890. While most of these accessories will be applicable to the top brands

A variety of feet and accessories are available for sergers, but they are usually specific to make and model. It's important to know what goes with your machine.

on the market, they are not all available for every brand. I've divided this chapter into two sections: overlock and coverstitch. For those with combination machines, it's likely that the coverstitch feet and accessories will be compatible. If unsure, reference your user manual or ask your local dealer.

OVERLOCK FEET

Typically, attaching and removing presser feet from the serger shank is a breeze thanks to the snapping mechanism located at the back of the shank. Most manufacturers include helpful markings at the front of the presser feet, denoting needle positions and, in some cases, the blade position. On a serger, needles move up and down and remain fixed in position, making it easy to use these markings as guides to maintain straight stitches. However, if the presser foot has a blade marking, it is intended for the neutral width, usually around 6.0.

When switching between different presser feet, it's recommended to consult the accompanying card or set of instructions. These materials provide suggested settings, such as stitch type, width, length, and whether the blade should be up or down. However, keep in mind that these settings are merely suggestions. Always test them out to ensure the needles and

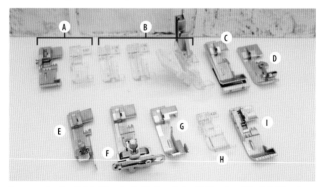

Some examples of overlock feet: two standard feet, one is clear (A), three clear piping feet, different sizes (B), gathering foot (C), cording foot (D), blindstitch foot (E), elastic foot (F), beading and sequin foot (G), clear curve foot (H), and shirring foot (I).

blade clear the foot properly. Feel free to experiment and have fun with your serger!

- **Standard:** Can also be referred to as the general foot, overlock foot, or overlock/combo foot. This is the basic foot that comes on all sergers but will be unique to each serger make and model. This foot can be used for both overlock stitches and coverstitches.
- **Clear:** The clear foot functions similarly to the standard foot, but with the distinction of being transparent instead of metal. Its plastic composition makes it lighter, which might require adjusting the pressure to a higher setting to ensure adequate fabric control. Increasing the pressure setting adds more force onto the fabric, aiding in smoother stitching. This foot can be used for both overlock stitches and coverstitches.
- **Piping:** This foot has a groove underneath, allowing a cord to feed under smoothly. To create piping, wrap fabric around cording and stitch both in one. This foot is also used to insert zippers with the serger—the zipper teeth feed under the groove similar to the cording. Depending on the make and model, this can come in various sizes; the BERNINA L 890 has a snap-on foot for 3mm cording, a snap-on foot for 5mm cording, and an adjustable, screw-on shank foot for 6mm, 8mm, and 10mm cording.
- **Gathering:** This snap-on foot is ideal for creating ruffles or gathering one layer of fabric to a smooth piece of fabric. To use this foot properly, adjust the length to the longest option and differential feed to the highest option.
- **Cording:** This foot is one of my favorites. It is ideal for adding thin cording, wire, or fishing line to the edge of the material. Think of wire-edged ribbon or the wavy hem on a ballgown. This is the foot to achieve such an effect.
- **Blindstitch:** Also known as a blindhem foot. Though originally designed to quickly and efficiently create a blindstitch on knits, modern serger pattern designers use this foot and the adjustable guide to create even-spaced rolled-hem pintucks and flatlock stitches for heirloom effects.
- **Elastic:** Sometimes referred to as the elasticator foot. The basic functionality of this foot is to quickly and efficiently attach elastic to the edge of fabric for various items, including lingerie and swimwear.

There are various screws on the foot for adjusting the width of the elastic and the amount of pressure placed on the elastic.

- **Beading and Sequin:** Use this foot to attach strings or yardage of beads or sequins, up to 6mm, to the edge of your material with an overlock stitch. When using a flatlock stitch, beads and sequins can be stitched down the center of the material.

- **Curve:** Due to the shorter nature of this foot, it works with both overlock stitches and coverstitches in stitching curves more accurately than the standard foot. When working with overlock stitches, it's ideal for stitching around the outside edges of curves, both concave and convex. When using chain and coverstitches, it's amazing in creating some lovely, curvy, decorative stitches.

- **Shirring:** Designed to work best with lightweight fabrics, this foot gently gathers a single layer of fabric along the edge with overlock stitches and down the center with either chainstitches or coverstitches.

COVERSTITCH FEET AND ACCESSORIES

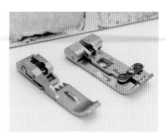

- **Coverstitch Foot:** As indicated by the name of the foot, this is used when stitching the coverstitch as well as the chainstitch.

- **Coverstitch/Compensating Foot:** This foot is ideal for stitching a coverstitch on materials with uneven thicknesses, such as multilayer bindings, hems with elastic tape, flat joining seams, or

The coverstitch foot (left) and coverstitch/compensating foot (right) are versatile for your coverstitch needs.

seams involving lace or elastic lace. Additionally, it offers versatility by allowing you to choose whether the needle thread or the looper thread is on top, enabling you to achieve different decorative effects.

- **Binding Attachment:** Designed as an attachment that holds and folds binding around the fabric edge, securing with either a narrow coverstitch or chainstitch. On some makes and models, an additional

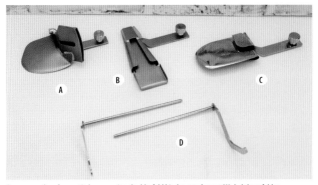

Some examples of coverstitch accessories: double-fold binder attachment (A), belt loop folder attachment (B), hemmer attachment (C), and two seam guides (D).

accessory holder is required for it to attach to the bed of the machine. Most often available for single- and double-folded edges.

- **Belt Loop Folder Attachment**: Sometimes referred to as flat binders and belt loop folder, these attachments are designed to hold and fold material toward the back, creating what looks like a belt loop. The material can also wrap around belting, ribbon, batting, elastic, and thick interfacing for purse straps. On some makes and models, an additional accessory holder is required for it to attach to the bed of the machine. Available in multiple sizes, depending on the make and model.

- **Hemmer Attachment**: Designed as an attachment that folds material toward the back, creating a hem secure with either a coverstitch or chainstitch. Some makes and models offer multiple sizes and the option to have the raw edge turn toward the front of the material. On some makes and models, an additional accessory holder is required for it to attach to the bed of the machine. Available in multiple sizes, depending on the make and model.

- **Seam Guides**: These typically come in a set of right and left. This is for stitching on either side of the presser foot and will slide into a hole on the shaft. Seam guides can be used for overlock stitching, chainstitching, or coverstitching, and they are designed to keep stitches evenly spaced and straight.

Get the Most Out of Your Serger

As you've progressed through this book, you've probably uncovered insights about your serger, or sergers in general, that have prompted you to reconsider their possibilities and applications. In this chapter, my aim is for you to discover effective solutions to common challenges encountered when using a serger compared to a sewing machine. Moreover, I hope to showcase the great potential that a serger holds, expanding your understanding of its capabilities and versatility.

START AND STOP

There are many differences between a sewing machine and a serger. This will become immediately apparent on your very first stitch. With a sewing machine, you usually lift the presser foot, slide the material under the foot, lower the foot, and begin stitching. While stitching with an overlock of any kind, you can start and stop whether on or off the fabric. On the other hand, while stitching a coverstitch, you will want to start and stop stitching on the fabric so the stitch can "lock."

Here are some basics on how to start and stop while stitching "in the round" with both overlock and coverstitch. Stitching in the round refers to serging a continuous seam around a circular or curved object, such as the hem of a sleeve, the neckline of a garment, or the edge of a circular piece of fabric.

Overlock

1. To stitch a continuous seam around a circular tablecloth, start by raising the presser foot. Remove the threads off the stitch fingers, pulling them toward the back of the machine, which will allow for the fabric to feed right under the presser foot without any threads being pushed to the side. Lower the presser foot.

2. Begin stitching all the way around the outside edge, cutting off little-to-no material; rather, just trim the edge. Stitch all the way around to cut the original thread tails. Very carefully cross over the original stitches by about ⅛"–¼" (3.2–6.4mm). Once finished stitching, lift the presser foot and pull the materials toward the back of the machine, once again removing the threads off the stitch fingers and allowing the threads to lay flat.

3. Clip thread tails with scissors or snips. The stitching will lay flat and smooth, providing professional results.

Coverstitch

1. To stitch a hem around a skirt, start the fabric at the desired position. Stitch all the way around.

2. Cross over the original stitches by about ⅛"–¼" (3.2–6.4mm). Once finished stitching, lift the presser foot, pull the threads toward the front of the machine, clip the threads, pull the material toward the back, and clip the remaining threads. This will lock the coverstitch.

REMOVE STITCHES

Removing serged stitches can feel daunting, but gaining an understanding of how each stitch is formed can greatly simplify the process. Let's divide this task into three sections: overlock, coverstitch, and chainstitch.

Overlock

The process of removing stitches applies to both 3- and 4-thread overlock stitches, ranging from rolled hems to traditional 4-thread overlock stitches. Understanding the construction of a 4-thread overlock is key; it involves two needles securing the looper threads that wrap around the fabric's edges. When you cut the "needle threads," the loopers will naturally release.

Using a traditional seam ripper, cut the needle threads every four to five stitches. Once the needle threads are cut, use the seam ripper to grasp the looper threads on both the top and bottom, pulling them out.

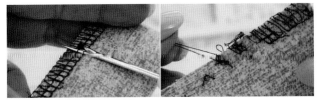

Cut the needle threads (left) and the looper threads will release (right).

Coverstitch

The coverstitch typically employs up to three needles that move up and down, securing the chain looper thread on the underside of the fabric. Similar to removing overlock stitches, once the needle threads are

Cut the needle threads (left) and the looper threads will release (right).

eliminated, the chain looper thread will naturally fall out. It's crucial to identify where your stitch began and ended.

To start, cut the needle threads every four to five stitches. At the end of the stitching, delicately grasp the looper thread and pull it out to complete the removal process.

Chainstitch

Removing a chainstitch is relatively straightforward, provided you can pinpoint where the stitch "ended." Flip the fabric so the chain looper is facing upward, then carefully use a seam ripper to grasp the chain looper thread. Gently pull it in the direction where the stitching ended, which will effectively remove both the needle thread and the chain looper thread.

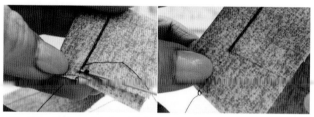

Cut the stitch end (left) and pull the threads (right).

AROUND CURVES

Regardless of whether you're serging on the outer or inner curve of a fabric, it's crucial to keep in mind that sergers stitch in a straight line, and they do so very well. Going around the outer or inner edge of curves will require manipulation of the settings or material. When going around either the outer or inner curve, the goal is to keep the fabric as straight as possible when the needle forms a stitch in the material. Here are some recommendations for effectively serging around both the outer and inner curves:

- **Curve Foot:** When serging around both outer and inner curves, consider utilizing a curve foot. As discussed in the previous chapter, this foot is shorter than the standard foot, resulting in less material being held down flat. This facilitates easier maneuvering of the fabric under the foot, aiding in smoother stitching around curves.

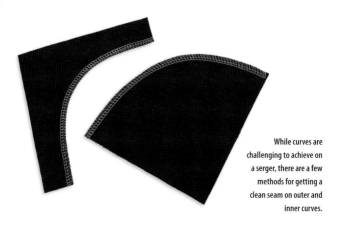

While curves are challenging to achieve on a serger, there are a few methods for getting a clean seam on outer and inner curves.

- **Differential Feed:** As mentioned in previous chapters, the differential feed on a serger allows for slight gathering when increased and for slightly pulling the fabric further when lowered. Playing with this setting can help materials lay much smoother.
- **Length:** Much like differential feed, adjusting the length while stitching on outer and inner curves can help keep the finished fabric to lay smooth and flat.
- **Pressure:** If the fabric seems like it is dragging, being tugged, or stretched out while stitching around an outer or inner curve, a quick fix could be to reduce the pressure.
- **Needle Up/Down:** If your serger has a computerized feature of finishing the stitch with the needle in the down position or in the material, this might come in handy when going around the outer and inner curves. This can help you reposition the material and have the needle hold the material in place. If your serger does not have the computerized feature, then simply turn the handwheel in the down position to secure the material.
- **Knee Lift:** If your serger is equipped with a knee lift, you might find it helpful to use when stitching around outer and inner curves, as it will allow your hands to remain free to make needed adjustments.

FINISH ENDS

While there are many ways to finish an overlock stitch, here I will cover the two most popular options.

Seam Sealant

Seam sealant is a type of liquid or gel-like substance used to reinforce and protect seams in fabrics. When you are securing your seam, leave about 1" (2.5cm) of a thread tail. Turn your fabric to the wrong side facing up. Place the corner or seam edge over a piece of paper to prevent any damage to your work surface. Place a small dot of seam sealant where the threads meet, whether

Use seam sealant to prevent raveling.

it's a corner or covering the threads at the end. Follow the manufacturer's instructions for dry time, and then clip the thread to the end of the fabric.

Feed Thread Tails Through Seam

This can be achieved with either a double-eye needle or the Lil' Hookey seam hook. When finished stitching the seam, leave about 1½"–2½" (3.8–6.4cm) thread tail at the end of the seam. On the wrong side of the seam, feed either the double-eye needle or the seam hook under the last 1"–1½" (2.5–3.8cm) of the seam, insert the thread tail in one of the eyes, and pull under, stitching so it lays flat. If this will be laundered, you might consider adding a dot of seam sealant to the end to secure it.

Weave thread tails through backside of stitching with double-eye needle.

Notions that Make a Difference

Similar to the specific tools and notions that aid in sewing, quilting, and machine embroidery, there exist essential items that significantly enhance the experience of using a serger. Presented below is a list of such notions along with their benefits when utilizing a serger, from left to right, top to bottom.

- **Angled Precision Tweezers:** These tweezers feature an angled design that facilitates grasping the end of a thread with precision. Additionally, they prove useful for removing lint from within a serger. My favorite are the Sookie Sews tweezers, which have a fine tip and angle perfect for sergers.
- **Hook Snips:** The hook located at the tip of the snips serves as a gentle means to grasp a single thread, aiding in tasks like removing stitches, clipping thread ends, and cutting threads during machine threading. I prefer the EZ Hook n' Snip Small Scissors by Sookie Sews because they are ergonomic, and perfect for both right and left hands.
- **Thread Snips:** Use any small snips to cut excess thread. But I use the Spring-Action Knife-Edge Thread Nippers by Gingher. These spring-loaded nippers are designed for slipping over one of your fingers, commonly the middle or ring finger, and comfortably held in your hand

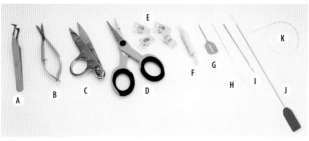

Angled precision tweezers (A), hook snips (B), thread snips (C), Zcissors (D), sewing clips (E), needle threader/holder (F), thread hook (G), looped needle threader (H), double-eye needle (I), serger needle threader (J), and serger looper threader (K).

during sewing. When it's time to clip a thread, simply grip onto the nippers and clip the thread tails effortlessly.

- **Zcissors by MADE Apparel:** These specialized scissors are crafted for precise cutting of coverstitch threads while securely locking stitches at the end. They boast rounded edges on the back of the blade for smoother thread sweeping and dual-side notches for snagging threads effectively. To utilize them: complete stitching a coverstitch seam, raise the needles to their highest position, raise the presser foot, sweep threads forward with the Zcissors, catch threads in the blades to cut, pull materials backward, and trim any remaining threads.
- **Sewing Clips:** Straight pins are not recommended, so as not to damage the blade. These handy little clips are ideal when working with a serger to hold multiple layers of materials together. My favorite are Wonder Clips.
- **Needle Threader/Needle Holder:** Many sergers will include a threader-holder combo; however, if your serger doesn't have one, there are multiple aftermarket options. The idea is that, on one end, there is a hole to secure the needle in the correct position for inserting into the machine, and the other side has a needle threader. Though they take a little practice when learning how to use, this is a handy serger notion you will not want to live without.
- **Thread Hook:** Features a hook for effortless insertion into the serger seam. Once inserted, it easily grasps the thread tail, allowing for smooth pulling through the seam to securely fasten it in place. I prefer Lil' Hookey because it has one slender end for the seam and one large end that's easy to hold.
- **Looped Needle Threader:** Perfect for threading both the needle eyes and loopers, this tool simplifies the process. Hold the needle thread and guide it through the large metal eye. Then, insert the pointed end through either the needle eye or the looper eye.
- **Double-Eye Needle:** This is similar to a hand-sewing upholstery needle; however, there is an eye on both ends. When using a serger, this tool is frequently employed to weave ribbon in a zigzag pattern on a flatlock stitch. Additionally, it's utilized for weaving the thread tails underneath the back of a serger seam.
- **Serger Needle Threader:** This manual needle threader facilitates threading the needle eye effortlessly. Ideal for hard-to-reach areas with needles and

loopers. A small metal wire pushes the thread through the needle eye, after which the thread is pulled entirely through using the small hook.

- **Serger Looper Threader:** Included with automatic threading sergers, these tools serve various purposes, such as assisting in threading thicker threads through the loopers, clearing lint from loopers, and bypassing the threading system. Resembling the Looped Needle Threader, this elongated metal coil features a loop at one end and a pointed tip. Simply thread the thread through the loop and insert the pointed end into the thread ports. For specific instructions tailored to your serger, refer to the user manual provided with your machine.

- **Machine Foam Mat:** Due to the higher stitching speeds of sergers compared to standard sewing machines, these mats prove invaluable for minimizing vibration, muffling the serger's sound, preventing bouncing and shifting, and safeguarding the surface during stitching.

- **Small Vacuum or Vacuum Attachments:** Always pull out lint and dust from sewing machines and sergers. When cleaning machines, it is recommended to use a small handheld vacuum or attachments that fit onto a larger vacuum.

- **Trim Bin:** Certain sergers come equipped with detachable trim bins, as discussed in preceding chapters. However, there are numerous aftermarket options available. Some attach directly to the front of the serger, tailored to a specific make and model, while others resemble thin plastic tables with a cutout housing a bag, which is emptied once full.

A trim bin (left) and a specialized vacuum (right) will help keep your serger in working order.

Maintenance and Troubleshooting

Maintaining cleanliness in your serger is crucial for prolonging its lifespan and ensuring optimal performance. This chapter will delve into essential maintenance and troubleshooting techniques to help you achieve just that.

Cleaning

Because a serger trims fabric edges during overlock stitching, it tends to accumulate significant lint. Cleaning your serger after each use is advisable to maintain its functionality, while scheduling professional servicing every one to two years is also beneficial.

Use the cleaning brush that comes with your serger to remove lint.

When cleaning your serger, it's important to avoid blowing into the machine, as this can increase lint buildup by pushing it further inside where it cannot be easily removed. Instead, utilize a lint brush and a small vacuum to pull out lint effectively. Moreover, abstain from utilizing canned air with sewing machines or sergers to avoid the risk of pushing lint deeper into the machine and the possibility of moisture causing rust within the inner workings of the machines.

Needles

While most home sergers can accommodate universal needles, there are specialized needles designed specifically for sergers, such as ELx705. The key distinction between "sewing machine needles" and "serger needles" lies in the structure of the needle's blade, which refers to the elongated middle section of the needle—not to be confused with the serger's cutting blade. Unlike sewing machine needles, serger needles feature grooves on both the front and back of this middle shaft. This design minimizes skipped stitches

Use needles specifically designed for sergers.

and ensures smooth thread movement, particularly crucial for handling the high speeds of a serger. While sergers can typically use various sewing machine needles depending on the fabric type, it's not advisable to use serger needles in a sewing machine.

Just like a sewing machine needle, for maintaining even, balanced stitches, it is recommended to change your needle every six to eight hours of use and dispose of the used needle properly. When replacing a needle, it's a good idea to place a small piece of paper or fabric under the presser foot. This precaution prevents the needle from accidentally falling into the serger if it slips through your fingers. Using a needle holder can certainly help provide stability and ensure the needle is positioned at the highest point in the needle bar.

Additionally, due to the close arrangement of multiple needles in a small space, it can be challenging to ascertain if the needles are correctly inserted and if the screws are securely tightened. Pay close attention to these details as they can impact the machine's performance.

Blade

Most sergers typically include a spare blade for replacing the original one when it becomes dull. The frequency of blade replacement depends on several factors, such as how often the serger is used, the types of fabrics being sewn, and the condition of the blade. Regularly inspect the blade for signs of dullness, nicks, or damage. If you notice frayed or uneven cutting, it's likely time to replace the blade. Some dealers recommend replacing the serger blade every 6–12 months with regular use. However, this timeframe can vary depending on the above factors. It's crucial to monitor the blade's performance and replace it as necessary to ensure precise and clean cutting.

Oiling

It's important to adhere to the recommendations outlined in your serger's user manual or guidance provided by your local dealer. Not all sergers require or are suitable for oiling.

Only oil your machine following the manufacturer's instructions.

Thread

In earlier chapters, we extensively discussed various thread types and their typical applications. As a general practice, it's advisable to safeguard threads from direct sunlight and dusty surroundings to prolong their durability, even when they're on the machine. Investing in a dust cover, whether provided with the machine or custom-made like the Dahlia Serger Dust Cover from Sookie Sews, can help protect your serger and the extension table when not in use. Moreover, aging thread may lose strength and become prone to snapping. If you're encountering frequent thread breakage, examining these factors could provide insights into potential causes.

A cover prevents sun from fading your thread and dust from getting into your machine while not in use.

Tensions

As mentioned earlier in this guide, threading and tensions often intimidate sewists and deter them from fully utilizing their serger. Whether you have a basic 4-thread serger or a top-of-the-line model, it's essential to remember that you're in control! Sergers are not as complex as they may seem at first.

While there are various factors that can affect stitch balance, they can usually be resolved with simple adjustments:

1. **Carefully rethread the machine**, ensuring you follow the threading paths precisely.
2. **Check the tension dials** to ensure they align with the manual's recommendations.
3. **Check needles.** Confirm they are correct for the material, are at the highest position, and that the width, length, and differential feed settings are all adjusted as advised.

After testing the stitch, if you notice threads pulling toward the front, it often indicates that the tensions for that specific thread/fabric combination are too tight on the upper looper. In this case, you can either reduce the tension on the upper looper or tighten the tension on the lower looper.

Most serger manuals include a basic troubleshooting guide for tensions. It's advisable to adjust tensions while stitching so you can observe the immediate effects on the thread/fabric combination. This real-time adjustment allows you to fine-tune the tensions for optimal results.

Tricky Materials

When dealing with challenging materials, it's wise to conduct experiments before stitching on your final project. Begin with the basics: use general serger thread, ELx705 needles, and the recommended settings outlined in the machine's manual. If issues arise, systematically troubleshoot by trying different needles, thread types, and adjusting settings such as length, width, differential feed, and pressure.

Once you've identified the perfect settings, create a sample and meticulously note down all the settings, including thread type, needle size, etc. Keep this information organized in a journal or binder for future reference. This documentation can serve as a valuable resource and guide as you continue to hone your serging skills.

Resources

In addition to the author's website (www.SookieSews.com) and YouTube Channel (www.SookieSewsTV.com), check out the following sources for inspiration, information, and helpful products.

Benartex Designer Fabrics: www.benartex.com
* Fabrics shown are from the Sookie Sews "The Beehive Bundle" from Benartex Better Basics and Cotton Shot by Amanda Murphy

BERNINA: www.bernina.com
* Machines used in book are BERNINA L 460 and BERNINA L 890

Clover: www.clover-usa.com

Dritz®: www.dritz.com

Gail Patrice Design: www.gailpatrice.com

Mettler: www.amann-mettler.com/en/

SCHMETZ Needles: www.schmetzneedles.com

Sulky: www.sulky.com

We All Sew BERNINA/bernette blog: www.WeAllSew.com

WonderFil Specialty Threads™: www.shopwonderfil.com

Y.L.I. Threads™: www.ylithreads.com

About the Author

Sue O'Very, affectionately known as Sookie Bee, brings her fresh style and love for sewing to enthusiasts worldwide. Known for her knack of simplifying sewing techniques, she makes learning memorable and accessible. Whether through in-person workshops, her YouTube channel, SookieSewsTV.com, or her online courses at SookieBeeAcademy.com, Sue is dedicated to sharing her sewing expertise with her community of Sewing Bees.

With a fashion design degree and years of experience, Sue teaches enthusiasts of all levels the art of sewing. Lovingly supported by her daughter Heidi and worldwide community of Sewing Bees, she continuously innovates to bring new sewing experiences to her audience. Join The Beehive Newsletter at SookieSews.com/TheBeehive to receive the latest updates. You can find her on Facebook and Instagram @SookieSews. As a thank-you for purchasing her book, visit SookieSews.com/PocketGuideToSergers for FREE bonus video tips.